SUNDAE POETRY

BY: Lauren"Lush"Collier

CONTENTS

CONTENTS

Cute/Sweet/Sassy/Imaginative

Dig Deep

Sundae Poetry

Written & Illustrated By: Lauren"Lush"Collier

<u>Dedications and Thanks</u>

I'd like to dedicate this book to the entire world, to my fans and fans to come.
I would especially like to dedicate this book to my deceased father (Joseph A Collier) who I love deeply and dearly. Words cannot express completely how I feel but with poetry it sure helps.

Big, big thanks to my family and friends because without support you tend to go astray from pursuing the talent God has given you. Special thanks to God for blessing me with the gift of writing poetry/songs and rapping etc... I love what I do and hope all of my readers do too! :)

Lush
(A Poem I Wrote For My Dad)

I pray to god and wish upon the stars...
That my sons and husband will be at least half the man
you are/
Daddy's lil girl it's tatted to the death of me....
And in all actuality you are the best part of me....
And I'm sensitive so with typing this I'm crying, pardon
me/
I'll give you every organ and all my breath so your heart
can always beat...
And you raised me well, wise and strong so I'm always
standing on my feet....
Gave me the encouragement to go for what I'm hungry
for and I'm always going to eat/
Believe in me, I'm going to achieve to be....
All the woman you hoped I'd be....
And your son is a genius, guaranteed to succeed/
In this world of no tomorrows we rise above it all...
I'll stay true to my love for you until the angels call...
Right now you're going through a setback, a lil down fall...
And you're going to get back on your feet even if at first
you have to crawl/
And that's not literally...

1

(Continued...)

Going to keep you proud daddy if not that would be so
silly of me...
You always taught me that knowledge was the key...
So I earned some and stole some....
Destined not to be dumb...
Screaming at the top of my lungs let there be freedom!
Let it ring...
And let there be light...
A soldier for a dad so we know you're going to fight/
Look it in the face tell it you aint never scared...
But if ever you are no worries I'll always be there/
I can really say I love you the most in this world
Eight-teen but always going to be your little girl/
Anything you want, you name, I got you...
I'ma hold you down for sure because you pop dukes/
I love you more than my sweet tooth...
And that's a lot so you know it's the honest truth.

Lush
"Fragile"

Oh so I'm the nutcase?
Can you relate?
Is the person you love the most deteriorating in front of
your face?
And you can hear the moans and groans in the next
room...
You could see the pain in his face from a distance, no
need to press zoom.
Fragile, can't say I know what you're worth now because I
been knew,
Ever since I shot my way out my mom's womb.
You see these wounds?
They're getting much deeper, and my pop's physical is
getting much weaker.
I'm a light sleeper; best believe I hop up quicker than
basketball sneakers,
to check on him.
When you know someone's trying their hardest,
It's only right to applaud them.
Have anything you want I can afford them.
This money aint shit to me, but you are my everything.

(Continued...)

If I could fit your shoes, you know I'd sport them,
But not as cool as you do, I'm thinking about you as usual,
on the regular.
Though life is pretty mediocre,
I'ma dawn on the good times, the laughs, the bonding,
And even Texas hold em poker,
Putting a smile on my face wider than the joker's.
I'm not much of a jokester but we're funny together,
And you know I'ma hold you down,
Whether the weather be stormy or too hot
Because there aint nothing a daddy's girl wouldn't do for
her pops. I'd describe him in a million words, but I only
need one...Outstanding!
Okay maybe a few more...devoted, heroic, pleasant,
Amazing, awesome, wonderful, delightful, brilliant!
and many more.
Forever it is you I adore, mi Amor.

Lush
"You Are the Heart of Me"

Seems like this world got a little bit colder...
Deep down I know you're not really gone,
It's just your physical that aint here no more...
But the pain sunk real hard to my core and my eyes aint
never, ever been so sore...
There couldn't be a greater father I'd ask for,
Because I adore everything you did,
From the business man to the raising of your kids...
I tip my glasses and raise my cup, to the father of the
year, every year, come on give it up...
To my pops', just give it up to my pops'!
(Sing)
I love you sooo, I'll never let you go...You are the heart of
me...
The biggest part of me...I know I gotta be strong and keep
living on...
You are the heart of me...
The biggest part of me... I love you sooo, I'll never let you
go...
You are the heart of me...
The biggest part of me....of me, of me.

(Continued...)

20 years I've spent with you, might not seem a lot, but a lot we've been through...
Through it together, no matter the weather you'd always brightened up my darkest days...
Life has so many crazy ways and sometimes we felt like getting away...
Pack up and go to a faraway place with no sorrows...
A better today and greater tomorrows...
I just have to know, is heaven how they say it is?
If so, if it's really true please save me a place right next to you...
I just want to smile for awhile....c'mon I just need to smile...for awhile.
Sing)
I love you sooo, I'll never let u go...you are the heart of me...
The biggest part of me...I know I gotta be strong and keep living on...
You are the heart of me...
The biggest part of me... I love you sooo, I'll never let u go...
You are the heart of me...
The biggest part of me...of me, of me...

(Continued...)

Daddy's little girl won't anything change that…
I'd give what I got just to bring you back…
But if you're pain free then daddy be free…
I'll never stop loving you until eternity.
Just continue to watch over "we"…
Mommy, Joey and me…
And forever we'll be grateful to have known you…
I know you're proud for the young adults we have grown
to…
We all really miss you and I promise to stay true to my
love, to my love for you…
We love u sooo…
We'll never let u go you are the heart of "we"…
The biggest part of "we."

Lush
"REFLECTION"

I met a woman today,
whom frowned from the inside and smiled on the out...
A woman who jumped for joy but seemed like she wanted
to shout.
We shared strong similarities, though her voice was
shaky,
And from a distance you would mistake her for me.
She said life has been good to her...
Looking very wealthy in pearls and a royal blue fur.
Diamonds that glistened like stars...
And the most latest and stylish cars.
Yet something was hurting her inside...
By the way she looked to the sky,
Like a lost butterfly...
When I asked for her name she gave no reply.
Reached for my hand...
I took hers, though I didn't understand.

(Continued...)

She then softly wrote nerual on my palm...
Remaining calm,
She showed me her heart...
Said how it fell apart...
The day her father passed (rest in peace)
I yelled "that's the missing piece,
that was torn!"...
But when I looked up she was far from gone.
I then realized it was me all along.
I met a woman today...
Strong and brave but hurt and lost...
And would pay any cost
To see her father's smile...
Love you daddy see u in a little while.

Lush
"Without you"

They didn't just take him they yanked him...
Heartbroken but it's double coated, painted...
You'd have to pick it up to really tell...
Since that day I haven't been feeling well...
No head cold, no I don't have a case of the flu...
I'm just sick, real sick without you...
Now I buy cases of brew...
Barely hang with the crew...
Because the only person I really want to see...is you...
Sometimes I get Déjà vu...
But I never saw this coming, these days without you.
Without you feels like these days aren't true...
That's why it's so hard not to write about you...
Ugh! Missing you.

Lush
"Hero"

Though it seems to get harder everyday...
I manage to keep my head where the clouds lay...
May be a little discouraged at times...
Not a stranger to being down, so up is the only way...
Familiar foot prints on the arch of my back...
They say "That girl is just fine," but that's not a fact...
Yeah I look well, but my insides are dying slow...
Losing the only one who really got me,
Got me flying solo...
And it's a lot of work...
Brushing my shoulders off but there's a lot of dirt...
Got a good, big ole heart but there's a lot of jerks...
Now I'm feeling like pops' was the only one that knew my
real worth.
Tears and cheers...
For the best person placed on earth...
At least in my eyes...

(Continued...)

Never had to second guess you were an angel, because
you wore no disguise...
And you still are...
No telescope needed, you'll always be my star...
Rising or falling...
Knew I needed help even when for it, I wasn't calling...
Your memory is where I run when I need to escape...
FOREVER MY HERO...
No mask, no tights, no cape.

Lush
"Memory Forever"

If I weep as I sleep
Please do not shake nor wake me...
For I am re-enacting good times with my father and would
truly hate to be bothered.
If I laugh or smirk a bit,
Or possibly throw a hissy fit
Please do not shake nor wake me...
For I am re-enacting good and bad times with my father
and would truly hate to be bothered
Needed lessons,
Sweet smiles and your distinctive voice I keep in memory
forever.

Lush
"Tinted"

   Tinted, hiding behind this here wall
Built from anger and hurt
Some huff and puff but it will not fall
For they are dirt and don't understand a woman's worth.

   Shielded from the childish games
From old lovers and meaningless flames
Some I can't recall their names
But on my heart u can still see the stains.

   Blocking out all unwanted memories
Left with only but a few
Wondering if some even remember me
For I was someone that you once knew.

   Ducking and dodging even from the innocent faces
Moving in the quickest pace
Maybe I was looking for love in all the wrong places
Man, it is so hard to fill this empty space.

8

(Continued...)

Please send me someone to love me for me
Because for so long I longed to be free
Please help me tear down this steel wall
And to not be afraid, in love, to fall.

Lush
"Stealer of my Heart"

Delicate sweets smell up the room
But my favorite treat is you
Caramel delight
So out of sight
Dimples I can stick my tongue in
You are such a dream come true
The constant thought in my mind
And stealer of my heart
I knew you would be mind blowing from the very start.

Seductive voice, my only choice
Dreamy eyes and plush lips
Butter soft skin and firm fingertips
You are the constant thought in my mind
And stealer of my heart

(Continued...)

The reason for my frequent cheesing
And the beating sound in my chest
My everything, my only
The love of my life
I dream to be your lovely wife
Holding one another each and every night
You are the constant thought in my mind
And the stealer of my heart.

Lush
"What Happened to the Love?"

Always seemed to reach for your touch,
But we never connect...
Distant from your kiss,
Yet our lips met...
Only a peck, nothing too deep...
Sometimes the bitter without the sweet...
Your fragrance lingers where you once slept...
The floor squeaks where you once crept...
A cold glass of water, or maybe a late night call...
Good, bad, ugly but I sure do miss it all...
A bad break up meant to us great make up sex...
But as of lately, not even a text...
Gone like yesterday...
Lost like a message in a bottle, wrapped in the sea...
Torn like a piece of you, like a piece of me...
What happened to the "there isn't any I, no you, but we"...
All thrown away over a couple of foul words?
A couple of flipped fingers?
A push, a shove? what happened to the love?

Lush
"All I Need"

Saw me on my worse day, swore it was my best...
Cleavage was peeking but you kept your eyes off my chest...
Cliché but you remind me of something that fell from above...
Your worse pick up line but I swore it was your best...
Pecks peeking I couldn't keep my eyes of your chest...
Your next move was your best move, a chess move...
You captured me as your queen, appreciate that boo...
Wonder if you saw my chest move...
Heart throbbing...
The way you stole it, thought you were mobbing...
No mask and gloves though
Just roses a bottle of rum and sweet nothings in my ear-drum...
Keep stroking my strings till I cum...closer
When I need to lean you'd always be my coaster...
On all four walls you're my only poster...

(Continued...)

No other face I wanna see,
Not even mine in the morning times...
Forget reading the times I rather read your mind...
So I could master the ways to make you all mine...
You're a mastermind, not the master kind you're to kind...
But I'd never walk over ya...
You'd be the soldier to my warrior...
Quick to put a dude on his ass...
Roughneck, but you left that in the past...
I don't mind bringing it back when you violating the back...side
Helmet attached to the head I'm always riding by your side...
Paradise is where I'm trying to reside...
Got me riding tides when I stare in your eyes...
When you stare in my eyes I still get butterflies...
Time flies when you're having fun, we must be going maximum speed...
What's your method man? How'd your love become all I'd need?

Lush
"Smart Heart?"

Begging to get closer to my heart than my skin...
But I'm afraid to let him in...
Cautious of it getting broken again.
He lets off a loud whisper like wind...
Many secrets remind me of how good of friends we've
been...
Treated love like it was a sin...
Though it isn't if it's done right...
Others make me dim; with you everything is so bright...
He said "for u I fight"...
"Never will there be fright"...
"For the love of you,
I'll take on a room full of gigantic dudes"...
I can go on, on how he delivers...
Claims to swim the longest river...
Ride the longest drive,
Just to get inside like honey to a hive...

(Continued...)

Though I want to let you know...
Though I want to let these feelings show...
I'm afraid you'll run,
and I'll be done...
For I am not down for the chase...
And how could I show my face...
How could I replace...
Bittersweet the taste...
So instead...
I hang my head,
and close my heart...
For it is the most fragile part...
To myself I say...
Maybe one day,
I will give him a call,
and give him, not some of me, but all.

Lush
"Lost love"

Dear: Johnny
My mind seems to roam
On these nights alone
Constantly checking the phone
As if you called and I missed it
I hate that we are so distant
Like our love never existed.
I fell down and you weren't around,
To help me off the ground.
You're across the coast
But now is when I need you the most...
Need for you to be close
My nights feel longer...
I can't take it any longer
Because this pain is much stronger.
If you can't come to me,
I will come to you...
I need you to see that my love is true

(Continued...)

I wouldn't give it a rest,
I have the address...
No matter if you're at your worse or best
See you soon Johnny.

Sincerely _Your lost love~

Lush
"No Nights"

Broken lights
On and off
And on and off
Broken lights
Deep cuts in my sole
Bleeding cuts in my sole
And if you look harder deep cuts in my soul
Stains get so old
Bed sheets so cold
Your body form still indented
Fragrance so gently scented
Rough nights
Feel better than no nights
Rather share bad times with you
Come back home for my love is so true
Will you?

Lush
"Nothing Last Forever"

Nothing last forever
So I try to enjoy every moment I spend with you
But you just enjoy every dime I spend on you
When we argue you say you wear the pants around here
But I pay the bills
While you play the streets
When I clean the sheets
You dirty them up
The same with the dishes,
The car and the bathroom
Give me good sex
But what's next? I ask you....
Another baby? another pair of footprint tattoos?
Can't take it, about to go nuts,
No cashew.

(Continued...)

I'm all about family
You're the cash rules everything around me type
Gossip gets you hype
I'm the see It to believe it type...
I don't hate,
But I've grown to dislike,
Every move you make
Every word you speak
Hate this weather, nothing last forever, can't stand the rain,
No poncho
So I want a divorce, like pronto!

Lush
"All Cried Out"

I think I'm all cried out...
This bottle of gin is all dried out
Hanging my head, moping around
Like a new trend I'm sporting this frown...
My baby left me alone
Now I'm stuck in a dead zone
I need to snap back to life and be strong...
I'm so far gone.
I can't get him out of my head,
like my favorite love song.
Show me the light,
Because I need to get through this night.
No more booze, he snooze he lose...
Thrown away like old shoes
"Whores or me?" I told him to choose...
And if he were to beg and plead,

(Continued...)

I'd just give him all he needs...
Toothbrush and underwear
For I'll be dammed to shed another tear.
I got too much to live for...
Now you ain't ever coming back through this door.
They say when one door closes, one opens...
Just be prepared when you leave your heart open...
For you might let the wrong one in...
Now taking precautions when letting a new Flame begin.
I'm all cried out.

Lush
(Just like that?)

Times are much worse...
Reliving this curse...
Groundhog Day, waking up to the same bullshit...
I wish things were different...
Aint cool how I mess up things and do it all over again...
My ink to this pen, my tonic to this gin...
Memories, thoughts of your nose tickling my chin...
The wind, as quiet as you were that day...
No clouds in my sky,
But tears filled your eyes...flood...
Hate ran through your blood...
You pulled the plug on us...
I thought we were so connected...
I know I screwed up, but, but you were supposed to
forgive me...
This sweet face, you couldn't stay mad at...
Bags packed, every item, you said that's that!

(Continued...)

What about me?
I'd follow if you wanted me to...
Beg, plead, all is what I'd do...
To be near, let's be fair...
I know you hate being lied to...
Slap my hand, time out; I'll stand in the corner...
A goner, like we couldn't revive you...
What happened to the future for "I do?"
Done, just like that?

Lush
"I must be"

I must be your jungle gym...
The way you run over me...
I must be the weakest player...
The way you pick everyone over me...
I must be your toilet bowl...
The way you defecate on me...
I must be nothing...
The way you don't appreciate me...

(To him)
I must be his angel...
The way he keeps me so high...
I must be someone special...
The way I give him butterflies inside...

(Continued...)

I must be first on his mind...
The way he runs to me...
I must be the apple of his eye...
The way he proposed to me!

Lush & Dave
"How Quickly We Forget"

Constantly told I'm far too kind...
It's crazy how rapidly things enter and leave one's mind...
But I once was, still am and always will be...
The man you once knew, still know and always will be...
Tussling for your love and respect...
Even buying it with gifts and checks...
Memories of the past and how I loved you so...
But damn it was all good just a week ago...
In my mind I ask what happened to us?
Oh so it's no biggie that your love decayed and vanished
like dust?
As what is dim needs to be made bright...
As what's in the dark shall always see light...
Trying to love your stubborn bones with all my might...
But sometimes I don't have the strength for petty fights...

(Continued...)

I guess in all actuality I don't know you and you don't know me...
It takes a lifetime to know and love someone and that's real spit...
Hoping and praying this isn't as good as it gets...
Through all the arguing, fussing, fighting and fits...
In the end we always say let's just be friends and that's it...
Minutes, hours, days, weeks go pass and wow "How quickly we forget."

Lush
"Fake"

How dare you borrow my heart?
Taking it for a spin...
Like a Jaguar or a Benz.
Gave it a nice paint job.
It felt whole and spanking new...
And when you were through...
Onto the ground you threw...it
Down came my heart...
Footprints indented...
I thought you would have gave me a life sentence,
Of love, love, sweet love,
But I was so wrong...
I felt so cold; with you I was so warm.

(Continued...)

The Jack to my Jill...
The capsule to my pill...
The bucket to my pail...
The walls to my jail...cell,
It felt so real...
But it was so fake.
Easily you moved on, me? I still mourn.
This once full heart, still torn...
Re-born.
I had to pick myself up and reassemble me.
You made me better because you didn't break me.
Stronger, wiser, swifter.
My eyes gaze and the heart follows.
In search for real love, with flaws and all.
Break ups to make ups...
I want it all, no holding back.
Him for me and me for him...
No games, just real love.

Lush
"Cup of Joy"

I don't need everything you got...
But I got everything you need...
An ounce of your love is a full cup of joy...
Smooth like cocoa, chocolate like chips ahoy...
I'm your honeysuckle...
On this love ride with my belt buckled ...
I aint never trying to fall off...
Yeah I bet the road aint nothing soft...
Still I put my all into this...
A few light bumps and bruises...
Moscato for the boat rides and cruises...
Tiny bottles of jack from the stewardess...
Oh how we love taking flights...
Even when I'm not touching land, your love is my highest height...
Don't mind if we fuss and fight...
Because the make-up love runs all through the night.

21

Lush
"But Then Again"

He's like the phlegm in my chest that I just can't cough
away...
Like a bad dream re-occurring every night and day...
But then again he's the beat to my ticker...
And the frame to my picture.
A confusion that leaves my heart unsure...
A killer shark that'll eat you to the core...
But then again a beautiful and rare sea shell washed
ashore...
He smirks when I hurt, but cry's when I cry...
He laughs when I fall, but helps me up so I could fly...
He ignores when I adore...
Adores when I ignore...
He still kisses me when I'm sick...
But then again, shoves me when I snore.

(Continued…)

He drives me extremely crazy…
But how could I ever leave my baby…
That man's a certified nutcase, who bugs me a lot…
But then again like deal or no deal, I'm sticking to the one
I got.

Lush
"Brand New"

Heart was on the pavement...
You picked it up gently...
Brushed it off and placed it back where it should be.
Though it cracked a bit,
You fixed it with your tender lips.
With your fingertips you nursed me back to health.
I feel brand new...
Like I could rule the world and you would be king...
Connected at the ribs, you never lower my confidence.
I write these words from the depth of my soul...
You put the tingle in my toes,
The arch in my soles.
Feels so right...
You swept me up and never let go.
Stole my sadness, replaced it with blissfulness.

(Continued...)

I'm on the verge of being whole again.
My missing piece...
Double chocolate treat...
Your love's my favorite song,
So I keep it on repeat...repeat.

Lush
"Who would have known?"

Can't stop cheesing...
When asked, I deny you're the reason.
Bashful, might take a lifetime to say how I feel,
So I pray my actions speak louder...
The clam to my chowder...
The happy to my hour...
The stem to my flower...
I know you will hold me up...
And I the same...
Hard doing work when you're on the brain...
But I get through...
Only minutes pass and I miss you.
But with all that being said, to another you belong...
Who would have known falling for you was so wrong...
Because your face read open, open for discussion...

24

(Continued...)

Flirtation, embracing your beauty...
I'd be the beast for I'd lock you away...
Only so forever you can stay...
Nothing but good loving I'd give you...
Don't take my love away I forbid you...
But you did do what I was afraid of...
This dream I will never let die...
I'll simply wait until you follow your fate...
And that's right here, loving me.

Lush
"Knocking To Be Let Out"

   Of course I'd like to write about other things,
But love seems to always find its way on my paper.
I could be angry or blue and there it goes again, knocking
to be let out.
Not like I've experienced a whole lot of loving...
But it just fills my heart, my mind.
I have so much to give, not a soul to give it to.
When I think I've found him,
He turns out like the previous jerk...
With hands and minds they flirt...
Chasing every curve and skirt.
Give up the goods too soon ...
And they throw your name in the dirt.
Call you a tease,
If you flaunt your lady lumps, but won't please.
It's like you can't win.

(Continued...)

Until that one day, that one moment occurs
And you actually meet the person you've always imagined
The one you always longed for.
That one person that loves all of your flaws.
That kisses your pale feet and enjoys it...
The one, unlike no other...
Whom without a broom, swept you right off your feet
With love in your eyes and love in his.
So when I find that very person, sweet and true
You will be the first to know,
For I will wear the glossiest glow.
Until then, my love is just knocking to be let out
Knocking and knocking...and knocking.

Lush
"Wonder"

Wonder if I'd gave my all would I've been left with
nothing when you turned the hall?
Walked away, the way you walk
When I tried to talk had me speaking in tongues
The first time we tongued breath arose from my lungs
A fresh feeling, but now you feeling yourself
Pockets swollen, you feeling your wealth
Heart stolen, I'm feeling my good health taking turns
The turns we take, mistakes we make, the breaks we took
The trust you broke
Left for broke, couldn't break me, I'm use to bending
Kind soul, I'm use to mending
Your use to pretending,
Use to hold me closely
Took a chance with you, was far too costly
Look what it cost me

(Continued...)

Hard to believe you crossed me, no dribbling
Hard to breathe when you divorced me
Bad penmanship... no signature required
Quiet, I need to hear myself think, though it's out loud
Isn't that allowed?
Not like I'm answering my own questions
Your last question
Can a young dude get money anymore?
Never stepped in the middle of that...
Riddle me that
You everywhere the ass and titties is at
Where they do that at?
Me? Oh I'm home
Frequently checking the phone
Not a ring, not a stupid ring tone
No nothing...so I call huffing, puffing
"The ring's on the dining room table
No fable, no bluffing"
But I was kind of bluffing...

(Continued...)

Came right home, "Babe you read my mind!"
"Been trynna tell you for quite some time, I gotta new
love, she prego and swear it's mine"
Jaw drops, heart stopped, but I gotta keep my composure
Head on my shoulders
Quick hands caught my heart
He was so happy it was over
Damn, I always knew he was a doldger
Glad I woke up, best part, no foldger
Staple this chapter, throw it in a folder
Never look back; maybe when I'm a little older, I'm sure
he'll be even colder....
Glad I aint give my all, aint have to worry about being left
with nothing, when he turned that hall
Hearts' where it need be, head to the sky...Yea that's me.

Lush
"Just 1 call"

As cool as the spring
Down for anything
My love don't cost a thing
But you can have all my cents...
Don't even need wisdom you can have all my sense...
Addicted to Your scent
Baby's so heaven sent.
Sent from above
Love that you don't judge...
Supporting my every move
Love the way you move
When we're in the mood...
We do what lovers do...
In the kitchen, in the pool,
While the kids are in school.

(Continued...)

Just One call away...
Your smile makes my whole day.
At the end of the night,
chocolate treats and candle light...
It's whatever you like...
Never really been the type,
But Let me cater to you.
You made me a better woman,
Your love's sweet like pudding...
And I sure do want it all...
In love with me is the only time I want you to fall...
Never too busy for you, I'll be there in just 1 call.

Lush
"Worthy of my Love"

Wish I could zone out...
But you hear me? Is constantly asked
Rather be left alone
Can't take the nagging
Rather let my mind breathe, not work overtime
Your troubles became mine.
I should have seen the signs,
And went in the opposite direction
But now I'm lost here, Stuck in this ditch
Wish I could ditch,
But I got a dash of hope that it'll get better
But when and where?
I need it to be now, when my head bursts
Would u sweep up the debris,
Or try to put it back together again

(Continued...)

Because though you get on my bad side
On your side I still ride
For that is what a real woman does
No matter if the man is up or down
Bent or straight...
Bent out of shape
We still give and give never really take
Only thing I take is the bullshit
And I take the time to try and understand
But tomorrow may be the day that I throw it all away
Now u can catch me in the act,
And straighten up yours, on all fours
But you gotta prove
That you're too good to lose
That your worthy of my love,
Of my love, of my love
For I might be gone by the time u stretch your arms
So treat me good for I treat you great
Loving you hard when those other chicks aint.

Lush
"Stranger"

Accustomed to this feeling that I feel...
Though I wish I wasn't...
We were closer than cousins yet as distant as strangers.
Never understood why and how you could hurt the only
one u said u loved...
At once your heart was purer than a dove and your voice
sweeter than a bird's
But this, I don't deserve...
This right here!
Deeper than a sword could ever cut...
A bullet could ever Pierce.....
This pain in my heart is taking a lifetime to disappear...
I just need u to acknowledge I am here...
And I won't go anywhere, but if you continue to push and
push,
While I am trying to pull,
Something is going to snap, something is going to break..

29

(Continued...)

Whether it be the trust, the love, the harmony that our heart's sang in,
But now my heart sinks in...
Hate that you put me down, yet still so comfortable in my own skin...
So in love with who you used to be
Now there's a stranger in the house and that stranger ain't me.

Lush
"Work it out"

Slammed doors
Broken glass
Slammed finger
Broken heart
Long scream
Blood stained screen
No picture on the TV screen
Many tears
Matching pair of footsteps
Heading for the hallway
No trail that you returned
3 nights 4 days
No call no show
Something's not right, like a sun with no light.
You usually return the next morning
Fed up with my constant calling
When I call it's straight to voicemail

(Continued...)

Where you at? No Nextel
The kids have questions,
I can't even lie I'm scared,
But I show them that I'm strong,
I show them how to lift up and carry on.
"Daddy's gone!"
My oldest tells the young ones
But I have hope
No suicide no rope
Couple of drinks, no dope.
Phone ringing I'm jumping like Double Dutch.
It's your friend Dutch,
Told me you got involved in some wild stuff
You're in the central bookings.
Be home in the night time
You called at the right time.
It was really my fault
I'ma make it up to you,
Do what a wife's suppose to do

(Continued...)

Bath ready, favorite foods on the table.
Kids tucked in
Tummy sucked in
Whip cream on the navel
Porno on the cable
I'm sorry
I promise not to flip again
Ralph, promise me you'll cool it now?
We could work it out
For the sake of our kids and the love we share.
Let's work it out.

Lush
"We"

What happened to the l.o.v.e that used to be in "we?"
The "I want to take care of you"...
Do all the things others wouldn't do...
Walk the moon...
You the fork, me the spoon...
The haters are the knives through our backs,
When we shine, over jealousy and currency stacks...
But not "we," we're tougher than that...
Deaf to the chitter chat, blind to the evil...
Insubordinate to the devil...
Burying the bones of the past, here's my shovel...
Dig it up to get another in trouble...
Nah that's not cool, so 6ft they lay...
Work hard but harder I play.

Lush
"Nice & Slow"

Dim those lights, just a little
And let's touch each other, just a little
Nice and slow, no need to rush
But if the alcohol takes over keep this on a hush.

Pucker up those lips, just a little
And let's kiss each other, just a little
Nice and slow, no need to rush
But if the alcohol takes over keep this between just us.

Grab the lotion and rub it in, just a little
And let's stroke each other up, just a little
Nice and slow, no need to rush
But if the alcohol takes over keep this on a hush

(Continued...)

Undress me with more than your eyes, just a little
And let's fondle and caress each other, just a little
Nice and slow, no need to rush
But if the alcohol takes over keep this between just us.

Lush
"Follow Me"

Follow me, follow me
I would never lead you wrong
Follow me to the hollow tree
Where we can sing our secret song
Follow me, follow me
There is so much to share
Follow me to the hollow tree
Let's race, bet I'll beat you there
Follow me, follow me
It's no one around but us two
Follow me to the hollow tree
You trust me and I trust you
Follow me, follow me
Let's share our first kiss
Follow me to the hollow tree
In ten years we'll reminisce.

Lush
"Crush"

The intensity of this crush...
So tempted to touch...
I'd yell it to the world, but I think I'll keep it on a hush
Because girls want what I want and I want you...
Sharing is caring but that I will not do
A kiss from your lips is so overdue
Hate repeating myself, but you I'd do...
All night long, the morning and the evening too...ooh
From the top of your head, to the top of your toes...
I'd kiss every inch, wishing time froze.
Pinch me I think I'm dreaming...
Just imagining touching you got me thinking it's real...
Got this hole in my heart that I just can't fill.
Phil was ill...
Juelz was cool
But none of them brothers got a thing on you...

(Continued...)

I can just picture the heights you'd take me too.
Over the rainbow surpassing the moon
Sweeps me off the feet with just one "good afternoon"
I'm in la la land when you speak my name...
The ooh to my la la...
The gucci to my goo...
The goo to my gaga.
Got me speaking gibberish,
I'm biting my tongue,
Because I want to say what I need to say,
But I'd be crushed if I can't have it my way...
And that's up!
Just you and I in a deluxe castle in the sky...
Oh my, oh my my my!

Lush
"Full"

Full
Like the curves of my hips
The width of my thighs
The feel of my lips
The tears in my eyes
Like the size of my breast
The sound of my moan
The pain in my chest
The tears in my eyes when nobody's home
Like the glass of red wine
The clouds in my sky
The sad thoughts in my mind
The tears in my eyes when nobody's home, but I.

Lush
"Mr. Mahogany Brown"

Mahogany brown, Mr. Mahogany brown
With those appealing lips
How could you wear such a frown?
If I were to caress you with my fingertips
Would you ease up and smile?
Share a convo over some dinner
Head to your favorite spot, man how it's been awhile...
In this love game I'm surely a winner.

Call me Mahogany brown, Mrs. Mahogany brown...
With your appealing lips
How could I wear a frown?
I love when you caress my chest with your fingertips
Mahogany brown
My Mr. Mahogany brown.

36

Lush
"Love a Man"

I like a man with good looks
But Love a man with a good personality.
I like a man who's tough
Love a man who's sensitive.
I like a man with a sense of humor
Love a man with great sense.

I like a man that likes to have fun
Love a man who takes care of business.
Not a fan of the cocky ones with the flashy rides
But Love me a man with confidence and pride.
Not a fan of childish boys
But boy, do I love a man!

Lush
"Tan man"

Tan man how do you wear it so well?
With your fitted denim and burnt orange beret...
The way you click your cowboy boots and sashay...
Through the crowded streets you go,
As if you were the only one to touch ground...
Whistling the most pleasant sound...
That tune that plays over and over in my head...

Tan man oh Tan man please tell me your name...
I feel a fool calling you what I do...
Who are you? Please do tell...
No worries on your face...
Not a wrinkle but older than middle age.
I'm so curious; I'd love to know your secret...
I am crushing so hard over your mysterious style...
Please stay and chat for awhile...

(Continued...)

He never said a word, never looked in my face...
He just whistled that pleasant sound,
That tune that plays over and over in my head.

Tan man oh Tan man...
I do not understand, I just want to get to know you...
I just want to walk with you...
Sing that tune, wear that tan and sashay these streets...
Though not a word left his mouth,
He grabbed my hand swiftly yet gently...
We whistled, walked and sashayed like we were the only
two that touched ground.

Lush
"From: Dad, to Daughters"

When it's hard and I feel weak,
I stand strong for you...
When I'm sad and I feel like there's no way I can get
through,
I just think about all the little things you do...
So special it makes me smile again...
I smile the brightest whenever you come around...
I must say that you sure keep your daddy proud...
Everything I do is for you...
I live my whole life just to protect you...
You mean the world and much more to me,
I adore everything about you, can't you see.
My angels from above and beyond...
You can have my heart if you want it,
Just be gentle, it's fragile...

(Continued...)

Can't see me living without you two...
My whole purpose...
On this earth surface,
Was to help birth the queens of my life...
Growing up in Queens seen much trife.
I can at least count two things I've done right,
Making 2, beautiful, young women.
 I'll be here from dusk to dawn, night till day...
Wake up and do it all again...
Just to see your face again...
I'll be there in just one call...
I'll be the ground if ever you shall fall...
In this life of games I sure did win...
THE BEST PRIZE OF THEM ALL!

Lush
"Drive Baby Drive"

Drive baby drive
Don't stop for red lights
For the drive is the honey to my hive,
Especially at nights

Drive baby drive
As my hair blows wild
You keep me so young and alive
Grinning from ear to ear it's been awhile since I smiled.

Drive baby drive
Drive fast, drive slow
Drive high, drive low
Drive short, drive long
Drive me all night long
Drive baby drive.

Lush
"Use Your Muscle"

    Hustle hard hustle hard...
Young girl hustle...
Girl pick up your head and use your muscle,
Not what's under your skirt, but what's under your skull
Lady, woman, not broad or dame...
You can be successful and still have the fame
Work hard and keep the dirt off your name
Promiscuous ones don't make it that far...
Don't be blinded by the dough, shine and fancy cars.

    Hustle hard hustle hard...
Young man hustle...
Man pick up your head and use your muscle
You can be wise, strong and make a whole lot of cash
Love and cherish your woman, don't be chasing the ass
Leave the drama to the dogs...
And death to the morgues.

(Continued...)

Do something constructive, get your name in the Forbes
Get on your J.O.B and earn clean money
Leave the drugs and the violence to the junkies

Hustle hard hustle hard
Young one hustle...
Keep that head up and use your muscle...
Be creative, come up with a positive hustle...
Hustle hard hustle hard...
Young one hustle.

Lush
"You"

Fifteen is becoming the new twenty-five
Blossomed shapes screaming I am alive!
Boys like girls
Girls like fancy cars
What happened to kids wishing upon the stars?
The sky being the limit
Follow your dreams don't be timid
Time waits for no one
Do it yourself don't depend on no one
A helping hand is always swell and grand
But watch out for the fakes
The high grass full of snakes,
Dying to get a bite
Of what you worked hard for
So be cautious of who you let through that door

(Continued...)

Make that money
Save that money
No need to brag or boast
It's usually the ones you keep close
That hurt you the most
Live life to the fullest
Dodging pot holes and bullets
Keep your eyes wide and your ears too
Be yourself at all times for no one can be a better you,
than you.

Lush
"Wrong/Useless"

Like a thoughtless mind
Still heart
Silent cry
Fruitless tart

Like a broken glass
Lost wish
Headless shoulder
Meaningless kiss
Like a dry cloud
Fake smile
Tamed crowd
Cracked tile

Wrong/Useless.

Lush
"Dreamland"

Nighttime used to frighten me
Afraid to dream
Because I'm having trouble separating them from reality.
It's like I'm having more fun,
More funds,
In my dreamland...
I don't think anyone else would understand,
So on the low I keep it...
My little secret...
Scaring the few men that I sleep with
Because I be singing and cheesing,
For no reason...
But I got a good reason
A great one at that...
In my dreamland I'm in love and I got a huge money
stack...

(Continued...)

Non-stop flap jacks and snacks...
And I don't gain an ounce of fat.
I see my dad and we share drinks...
We play go fish, and go fishing in minks...
Having the time of my life
Till it's time to go back to my real life...
Full of guns, drugs and trife
Pregnant kids, knives and angry wives.
So after a hard day at work,
I rush to my bed to clear my head.
Hello dreamland! Oh how I missed you,
The only place where there's no drama and issues.
My perfect world
My dreamland.

Lush
"Only Human"

Behind every jerk there's a nice Guy
So behind every nice Guy there's a jerk, maybe
But one can become at any giving minute,
For we are only human.
Behind every brave soldier
There's a timid kid
So behind every hero there's a shy, hesitant person,
maybe
But one can become at any giving minute
For we are only human.

Lush
"Silence"

Silence, it's been so long since you've come around...
Haven't seen your face in awhile, pal.
Wow! Feels good to dance with you, your lead...
Singing the same sweet melody.
I whistle, you whistle twirling simultaneously, as if we
were one.
When you're away I long for your presence...
Stretching my neck to see if you were on your way.
Calling your name three times, but nothing...
Not a squeak in the floor, a shadow on a wall.
A distant memory you remain...
Until the rain came this evening and you appeared.
You silenced the drops...
Made all of the pain stop.
All of the fast thoughts slowed down.

(Continued...)

Up is how I feel when you're near, dear friend of mine...
Silence how I am so saddened to see you go astray...
I shall gladly hum our tune until you come back one day.

Lush
"Sisterly Love"

Chipped shoulders we cry on...
And it be the ones we really rely on...
That turns up their nose like a bad smell.
Cold shoulders, face drops, tears hit the ground...
Sounded like thunder and boulders...
Parents hold us...
But sometimes it takes more than a hug...
A chronic tug at the softest part
Strong but quickly can be torn apart, the heart...
Over a man or a tenth of a grand...
When younger we had plans...
But it wasn't the man's plan...
Before the jealousy and disagreements
Used to be a perfect fit...
What happened to the love, I was the hand,
you the glove...a perfect match...

(Continued...)

One hand wash the other, the other scratches the back...
How could we find a better bond than that...
Now it's kind of strange when we exchange change...
You've changed or maybe it was me, we've...
Grown apart, grown up...
But never crossed that path...
Never ignored a call...
And no matter how far, I'll always be the ground if ever
you shall fall.

Lush
"Lifestyle"

Ever just feel like u don't belong?
Might have took a wrong turn on that long road to screw
ups and heart break hotels.
Obstacles the size of giants
And if you go under can you get back up?
Head to the ground, you better pick that up
Dirt on your favorite slacks and shirt, you better dust that
off...
Didn't think life would be so hard, but momma never said
it would be soft.
Nope, tell you to pull yourself up but never lent the rope...
Use to have a Dirty mouth, but never tasted the soap.
But definitely tasted some tears
Some Jack, some beers...
Fought some animals? No, never lions, tigers or bears,

(Continued...)

But what's the difference...
They're all trying to tear you apart,
Eat you alive
That's why, I will survive
Always plays in your head
Parents preaching to you always stays in your head.
When they do it so constant
The struggle's so constant
That bullshit, that nonsense.
Someway, somehow you have to find what works for you.
Start your own business,
Have hard workers work for you,
Or do the typical 9-5
Shitty pay but it gets you by
Shitty marijuana but it gets you High.
Found a mate, not your dream candidate
But they make you laugh and smile

(Continued...)

So you let them stay forever not just for awhile.
The bells ring
The kids sing
And you grow old
Though life was rough, never sold your soul
Never stabbed your best friend for a piece of that gold.
Just kept it real
Though it wasn't the best hand to deal
Took it and shaped it
Couldn't erase it
But took bad memories and replaced it.
Smiley faces when you awake now
Trusting everyone in your surroundings, no more covering
your plate now
A round of applause for your lifestyle
Big round of applause for your lifestyle.

Lush
"When the Cookie Crumbles"

Don't look for me when the wall tumbles...
Don't ask for help, you poured your own troubles...
Don't assume you can use my broom when the cookie
crumbles...
You failed to listen when I warned you that out there's a
jungle.

Always had your back always was there on the double...
Don't look at me as foul; I'm not the one who stung you...
I put the good ole ball in your hand; you turned around
and fumbled...

Thought life was a joke...
Until it had you in a snug hold like a choke...
Drenched in sorrow, use to be my kinfolk...

49

(Continued...)

Now we estranged like divorces...
The forces of evil got you hearing voices, trying to deceive you...
Home should be where your heart is, your kids really need you...

Drugged, bugged now you in Bellevue...
I done lent my hand a million times and you pushed it away a million more...
I use to feel for you but that washed ashore...

Who am I kidding, though I say it, I can never give up on you...
I can never say we're over and through...
No matter how hard this is to endure...
Look for me; I'll always be the one with the open door...
Forever, and ever and ever.

Lush
"Real Life Woman"

Peaches ~N~ Cream...
Butter pecan Queen...
Some or everyman's dream...
Funny, sexy and everything in between...

Sassy and classy...
But will drink you under the table...
Gifted and swift, if you ask me...
Real life woman, no tale, no fable...

Daddy's angel...
Mommy's demon...
Heart in a tangle...
Fighting for freedom...

(Continued...)

No fun being locked away...
Waiting for my king or prince charming...
Hoping to be freed someday...
Whom is tough as nails yet soft as Charmin...

Lush
"Keeper"

Street clothes on, hanging with his peeps...
On closed streets, he peeps me but doesn't speak...
His eyes are doing all the talking...
Staring on the low while his boys are gawking...
I see he's a little gentle unlike the other men...
Steps up smooth "will I ever see you again?
Because you looking right miss, you should be my miss
right"
Hoping he wasn't coming on too crude, but it was all
good...
I like n*ggas with attitude (N.W.A)...In a good way...
He was getting clean money, that good pay...
A dreamer, microphone fiend and a DJ...
All wrapped in one...
Smart and funny like a joke, what else can I say ...

(Continued…)

The complexion, don't get me started on the physique…
Biceps popping, no flexing, pearly whites…
Bowlegged, Levis with the all whites…
Looking beyond scrumptious…
A model was my first assumption…
Good fella wasn't part of the corruption…
Looks aren't everything it's much deeper…
But he got it all, a true sweeper…
How he got me floating…
Blunt, frank, real no sugar coating…
He's a keeper, so I'ma keep him.

Lush
"Rolling stone"

Fitted cap back, cruising...
Rolley on the wrist...
Comedian friends, something's always amusing...
Crib, car, money doesn't get better than this...
Fast life...
Shorty on my side, but not the wife...
She at home with the lil one...
Controlling, she aint allowed any fun...
99 problems but a b*tch aint one...
Big things popping, plenty of funds...
Sprees, shopping, wheels at a freeze but the rims aint stopping...
They say "that boy fly/flee"...
Catch me in the sky, no flights...

(Continued...)

If me and wifey ever fight,
I aint coming home that night...
I'll be with the other chick,
Slim waist, thighs super thick...
I'm a rolling stone, rolling stone and I like it!
Momma ashamed of me...
Said she disowned me, she aint claiming me...
Wife said I aint turn out to be who I claimed to be...
A gentle man, ha! She's too funny...
Should have known the only thing I love is my money...
I'm a rolling stone, rolling stone and I like it!

Lush
"Dear Cancer"

<u>Dear: Cancer!</u>

I cannot express how much I hate you...
Fighting back tears as I type...
Just speaking your name has me amped and hype...
You've hurt too many families and it just isn't right...
How could you be so gruesome, so destructive and cruel...
Crawling in bodies, using us as a tool...
I wish upon a star everyday...
For you to pack your bags and go far, far away...
Never to see your face again would mean a whole lot...
Just dig yourself a ditch, hop in it and rot, and then rot again!
Let me calm down before I disrupt the public...
Pain, pain go away, need a little something to numb it...

53

(Continued...)

Took my papi, and my cousin, shit I'm so vexed...
Let's make an agreement, sign your name by the x...
Leave my world, create your own and just live by yourself...
We don't need you here, never did never will...
You got the looks and you literally kill...
Poof be gone...finally in peace we will mourn.

Lush
"16 years young"

   Sputum and blood splatter the cold floor
He yells do what you're told, or you're going to get sold!
Struggling to lift thy head, she looked him in his face
Eyes so cold so deep
She wanted to do nothing but swear
But her tongue she holds
Be a good girl he whispers and softly pecks her on the
nose
Shamelessly she soils her clothes
Hoping no one knows
She washes up quickly, hates being filthy.
For many men she dances and bends.

   Troubled girl about 16 years young
Stutters her words but swift with the tongue

(Continued...)

Foul mouth since she could speak,
There's no change in that, didn't finish school
Claimed there wasn't any change in that.
Her boyfriend didn't split when he found out that she
strips
He just invited his friends and picked up all the tips
She was pissed, but time ticks and ticks
So when he came out his lips she put slits in his wrists.

    Sad girl about 16 years young
Never been a scholar
Known for running away from home
Two parents and a brother
Love her to death
Nearly lost their breath
When notified of her death

(Continued...)

Left a note that read:

 "Dear god and family, forgive me for I sin
but I cannot right my wrongs for I have so many
I cannot turn back the clock, for time waits for no one.
Don't cry for me, just celebrate,
For I'll be back to do it the right way.
Well I love you all but I've got to run
I've got a gallon of gin and a bullet in this gun
Russian roulette, let's see if I'll beat the sun."
                                        Love Amy.

Lush
"Fast & Hurt"

Butter boned, cherry hair...
Polka dots on the arch of cheeks...
Teeth like the skin tone, cracked lips like chipped paint...
Powder blue eyes, lids painted purple and gold...
Blood stained on the left as if the dye left traces...
Cold, hard...
Irreplaceable, non-duplicated, non-refundable...
Bad habits get the best of one...
Some features still glowing while others pale...
Frail and lifeless...
Many males never stayed...
Never awoke to hear
"Good morning beautiful, coffee or tea?"
Dollar bills or not, dirty sheets and ripped clothing...

(Continued...)

Cologne lurking on the opposite side of the bed...
Mixed aromas, Bobby wore Tommy, Fred wore Sean and
Elvin wore Ralph...
The rest got erased like they will soon...
Fast and hurt...
Depressed, constant sobber, sober only in dreams...

Once precious, still quiet, still hurt...
Alone, used, the user, abused and the abuser all in one.
Fast and hurt, many faces she wears...
Where's the face of courage and hope?
She lost that years back...
Finding it is hard and long but the journey and strive
Is well worth it.

Lush
"Down for the ride"

How could you come along for the ride but not ride to the finish line?
I could give you everything you'd ever need if you were only mine, but I know that will never be...
So I'ma keep it moving like leaves on a tree,
When that wind blows and oh,
I aint never have nobody treat me quite the way you do.
The way you stare at me makes me feel so beautiful,
But knowing that you're someone else's is so crucial...
to me
You were so perfect to me...It was all worth it to me.
All I ask is for you to never forget me
Just smile and laugh at all the times you smiled and laughed with me...

(Continued...)

I'ma hold you down still,
Because in a couple years I do feel,
That we could reunite and make it right,
But it might... just be me wishful thinking again...
And I don't want to be lost in the wind,
But often I get lost when I'm thinking of him,
You know thinking of you...I kept it official for you,
Now I need boxes of tissues when my friends start
mentioning you.
At first you'd give me anything I want,
I'd just have to point to it...
Hope I wasn't just a pencil to you,
Something you can use and use until there aint no point
to it.

(Continued...)

Throwing me away or pushing me off to the side...
I know it would be her if you had to decide...
So I'm not going to waste whatever time I got left
Just know I think of you with every depth of my breath.

Lush
"Cold Tears"

Cold air, cold tears
Tissues everywhere
Carpet bleeding
Mama's screaming, please let me be dreaming!
That man's coming
I hear him humming the same song
The night grandpa was gone
I reach for my father who's grabbing my brother
Who's hugging my mother
One hand on each other, together forever
Him, take us? never!
Cold air, cold tears
But we make it out together.

Lush
"Get Well Soon"

When life gets real tough...
It's hard to hide it or bluff...
When it seems like your best isn't enough...
Although we haven't been our best in awhile...
We still manage to laugh, love and smile...

The days are long and the nights seem colder...
When young we rush to get older...
Now we hold on to every second...
Cherishing it like a delicate memory...
Giving the tightest squeeze you ever gave...
Still brave and no matter the agony
WE WILL NOT CAVE!

Lush
"I'm Alive, I'm Alive!"

I'm alive I'm alive!
Don't walk over me...
My heart is beating like yours...
Can't you see, can't you see!
Why don't you acknowledge me?
I'm wise like you, strong like you...
I've got legs, lips, arms like you.
I'm here...I'm here!
See? See those are my footsteps in the sand.
That's my heart beating so fast.
Half of my heart on my sleeve...
Can't you see, can't you see!
It's falling, it's breaking!

(Continued...)

I'm alive I'm alive!
Don't walk over me.
I'm here...I'm here! I did not disappear
I sing, I dance... I long to be free.
Don't you have pity,? Have mercy for me?
Don't walk over me...
For I might just grab your feet and make you like me.
Dust in the wind...In the corner of a room...
On a bristle of a broom.

I'm alive I'm alive! Can't you see, can't you see!
Don't walk over me, or I'll make you like me...
I'm alive I'm alive!
Don't walk over me...why won't you see?
I don't ask for much...just acknowledge me.

Dave
"This is where I Live"

Where I live is a deep bottomless pit of depression...
Another blunt, another session...
A bill, a task, I just keep stressing...
But all things learned in life are lessons...
I tend to wear my heart on my sleeves...
An opened wound in my heart, so I tend to bleed...
But it's all about the love of my seeds...
I ask god for what I want but he only gives me what I need...
There's no room for failure so I must succeed...
I must stay upright, though I need air to breathe...
Trapped in a dungeon; which I call my mind...
Simulated by a world that is just as unkind...

(Continued...)

Humanity is lost, there is no love left to give...
All my letters read; return to sender...
Please just put "This is where I live."

Lush
"What's Life?"

What's life? If at any time it can be taken away...
What's freedom of speech if we can't say what we want
to say?
When we fight for what's right why do they put us in jail?
Knowing that families are just getting by how are they
going to make bail?
I don't understand a lot in this world...
Feels like there's a lost soul in this lost little girl.
Only thing I really know is the streets...
Gossip on who has beef and who packs heat.
Death? I'm not scared of it,
Because it's going to come whether you like it or not,

(Continued...)

Heaven is life and hell is hot.
What's life?

Lush
"Rotten"

Bad ones fall beneath your steps like rotten leaves...
Odor turns heads as if they were the living dead...
No color, no joy, no face...
No warmth, just a bad after taste in thy mouth...
A bad vibe in the pit of your insides...
Just moans, no cries, no laughs...
Still, like a pole, like a lamp...
Late nights pouring your soul into their well...
Tell a joke, sing a song, no lips crack...Liveliness, you lack...
Huffing and puffing as if you hated being near...
A few pinches, no budge, no emotions...
Still, stuck, bland, boring, dull, bad...Rotten.

62

Lush
"Don't Mistake my Kindness for Weakness"

When you knocked me down with your harsh words
I sprung up, but suddenly fell back like a hurt bird.
When you told me you loved me yet still walked out
I had so much to say, but no words left my mouth.
When you pushed your fist on my face
I slowly staggered out of place.
But when you roughly touched my son
I got over heated like a flaming sun
Oh, how fast you can run
This relationship is so far over and done...
For you have crossed the line

(Continued...)

And though I let you think you won all of the other times...
At the end, victory is mine...
Love might be blind
But I am no fool
You just lost the best thing you ever had, times two!

Lush
"Love in a Form of a Token"

She yelled "who needs A HEART when a heart can be
broken!
Just give me your love in a form of a token"
With opened hands and a shielded heart
So afraid of cupid and his dullest dart
Dodging relationships & love bugs
No matter a gentleman or a sweet thug
Been through it all, she claims
Different face and style but they're all the same
So at the end of the day all she wants is the change
"Don't baby me this, don't baby me that,
You don't stand a chance unless your wallet's real fat"

(Continued...)

Many Years pass and she's still the same
45 playing the same ole game
Her health was bad, been through so much pain
Felt kind of sad when I heard her name,
On channel Nine News
At first was so confused,
On the cause of death.
She yelled "I love my money" then took her last breath
And at the wake, there was no one there
Damn, the funeral too
I guess even though you love money,
Money doesn't love you.

Autobiography

Lauren Collier aka Lush was born and raised in Jamaica Queens NY on August 28 1989. She fell in love with music at an early age and started out writing and reciting rap songs. In 2010 Lauren became more focused on writing poetry, she then began to put together her poetry collection to create her first Poetry Book "Sundae Poetry."

"To my fans and fans to come, I truly hope you all enjoy this book as much as I enjoyed writing it. I love to express my feelings through poetry and songs and I thank you for supporting me and my dreams of sharing my words with the world."
-Lauren Collier